DON'T
Poke a
WORM
till it
WRIGGLES

For Charlotte
in memory of many charming worms

First published 2014 by A & C Black,
an imprint of Bloomsbury Publishing Plc
50 Bedford Square
London WC1B 3DP

www.bloomsbury.com

Copyright © 2014 A & C Black
Text copyright © 2014 Celia Warren
Illustrations copyright © 2014 Sean Longcroft

The right of Celia Warren and Sean Longcroft to be identified as the author
and illustrator of this work has been asserted by them in accordance with the
Copyrights, Designs and Patents Act 1988.

ISBN 978-1-4729-0023-4

A CIP catalogue for this book is available from the British Library.

Printed and Bound by CPI Group (UK) Ltd, Croydon CR0 4YY

1 3 5 7 9 10 8 6 4 2

MIX
Paper from
responsible sources
FSC® C020471
www.fsc.org

Celia Warren

DON'T Poke a WORM till it WRIGGLES

Illustrated by Sean Longcroft

A & C BLACK
AN IMPRINT OF BLOOMSBURY
LONDON NEW DELHI NEW YORK SYDNEY

Contents

Book Worms

If this book wriggles
and squiggles and squirms,
that is because it's a
book full of worms.

Curl up like a worm
and enjoy all the rhymes,
a hundred, a thousand,
a million times.

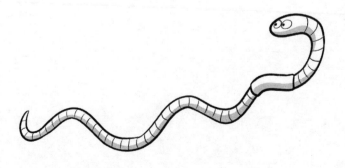

Don't Poke a Worm

Don't poke a worm till it wriggles.
Just joke with a worm till it jiggles
and breaks into chuckles,
goes bendy and buckles
and giggles and giggles and giggles.

Hey Wiggle Wiggle

Hey wiggle wiggle
The worm had a wriggle,
He squirmed right over the mole.
The little mole gaped
To see he'd escaped
And the worm wriggled into his hole.

Sing a Song of Squiggling

Sing a song of squiggling,
A garden full of worms,
Four and twenty sneezes
Cover them in germs.
When I dig the flower-bed
The worms begin to squirm,
Why am I allergic to
The humble garden worm?

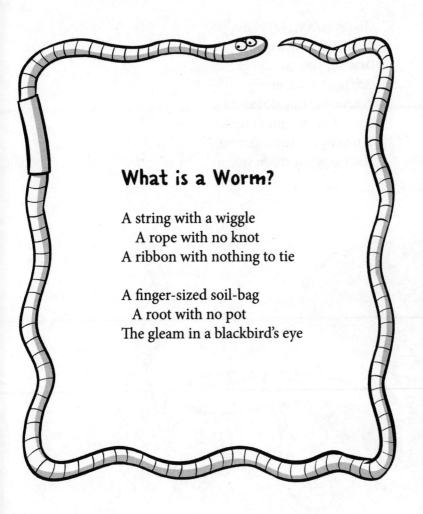

What is a Worm?

A string with a wiggle
  A rope with no knot
A ribbon with nothing to tie

A finger-sized soil-bag
  A root with no pot
The gleam in a blackbird's eye

11

Tweet Tweet, Blackbird

Tweet tweet, blackbird,
Have you any worms?
Yes, sir, yes, sir,
My beak squirms:
  One for the robin,
    One for the thrush,
And one for the nightingale
That sings in the bush.

If I Could Choose

If I could choose what I might be
I'd like to be a worm.
And no-one would say 'sit still' to me
If I could choose what I might be.
I can't sit still, you must agree:
I wriggle and I squirm.
If I could choose what I might be
I'd like to be a worm.

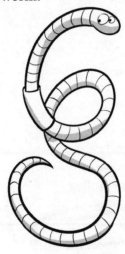

Wonderful Worms

Anna Worm is acrobatic,
Bertie Worm is brave,
Charlie Worm is cheerful,
a daring worm is Dave.

Elspeth Worm is elegant,
Freddie Worm has fangs,
Gertie Worm is simply great,
Harvey Worm just hangs.

Ivy Worm's inspiring,
Jasmine Worm, she jives,
Katy Worm is kindly,
Lucy Worm saves lives.

Mary Worm's magnificent,
Nasreen Worm is neat,
Oliver Worm is odd at times,
a popular worm is Pete.

Quentin Worm is quiet and quick,
Richard Worm is wriggly,
Sanjit Worm's surprising,
Tamsin Worm is tickly.

Ulrica Worm is upside down,
Vikram Worm is vexed,
William Worm is witty and wise,
a secretive worm is X.

Yolanda Worm likes yellow sand,
Zoe Worm has zest.
Ask any worm, "Are you wonderful?"
and all worms answer, "YES!"

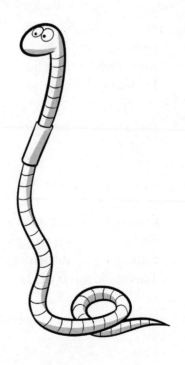

Wormy, Wormy, Oh So Squirmy

Wormy, Wormy,
Oh so squirmy,
How do your segments coil?
Through eating clay
And sand each day
And forty sorts of soil.

Through a Window

One day a worm looked through a little window
  and saw a starfish, far from sea or sand,
But the window was the glass of a jam jar,
  and the starfish was a small boy's hand.

Ark Anglers

Noah let his sons go fishing,
only on the strictest terms:
"Sit still, keep quiet and concentrate:
 we've only got two worms!"

Reliable, Pliable Worms

Worms are dependable
  stretchy and bendable
always extendable
  never expendable
garden befriendable
  completely commendable:

Give that worm a medal!

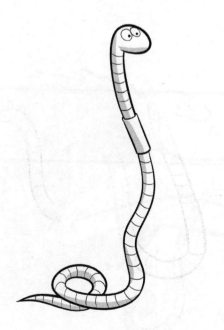

The Worm that Turned

O
here is
the
worm
that
turned
but
not
the other cheek,
this
worm
wrapped
himself
around
the
early bird's
fat
beak.

Weeny Worm Wuffet

Weeny Worm Wuffet,
Squirmed on a tuffet,
Eating her soil and clay.
A hedgehog appeared
With a prickly beard
And frightened Worm Wuffet away.

One Famous Worm

My name is so famous that, maybe, you know it:
I'm William Wormsworth, a classical poet.

Another Famous Worm

Leonardo da Vormi, an Italian wormy,
could writhe his name backwards, the teaser!
One of the cleverest worms on earth,
he painted the Squirma Lisa.

Late Worm

When my worm snuffed it
somebody stuffed it:
Taxidermy
can be wormy.

Small Robin Horner

Small Robin Horner
Sat in a corner
Eating his fresh worm-pie.
He stuck in his beak
And flew into next week
When a worm whipped him right in the eye.

If Worms Were Wishes

If worms were wishes
I'd dig every day
and fill up a bucket
of worms on the way.

I'd pick up each one
and, worm after worm,
I'd make lots of wishes
to make people squirm:

For Tommy (who pushed me
and trod on my toes)
I'd wish he had worms
hanging out of his nose.

For Polly (who stuck out
her tongue at me earlier)
I'd wish her tongue longer,
and thinner and curlier.

But for Mum (who has loved me
since the day I was born)
I'd wish extra worms
in her lovely green lawn.

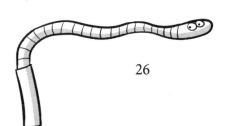

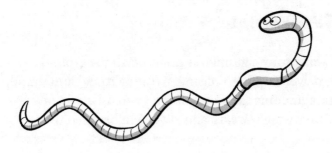

News Item

"The scientists know everything about me,"
said the worm, as it wove down one more hole,
And its five tiny hearts beat faster,
"But they still don't know about my soul."

Flexi-Worms

Twenty soily centimetres underneath the ground
flexi-worms are exercising, writhing round and round,
strengthening their muscles in gymnastic pursuits
as they wiggle-weave and zig-zag in between the roots.

Tiptoe on the grass, now – don't make a sound;
mustn't wake the worms up deep underground:
worn out with work-outs, they're curling up to sleep
thirty dirty centimetres underneath our feet.

Sssshhhhh!

Vermicular* Olympics

Ploughed field events:
Long stretch
High stretch
100-segment wriggle
Squiggle, wiggle and curl
Pebble-put

Puddle events:
Back squirm
Saddle squirm
Caterpillar squirm

(*of worms)

Elf and Safety

If you're a worm never visit the home
of a fairy, a pixie, an elf or a gnome.
They'll ask you to stay, in fact, they'll insist.
And how will they use you? Consider this list:
  As . . .
a beetle's lead – for walkies,
a skipping-worm – for play,
a worm to tie their hair up
if it's getting in the way,
a guard-worm, in holly leaves,
or, laid out on the floor,
a living draught-excluder
shoved up against their door,
a worm that's slung between two sticks
for washing to hang on – a worm in a fix!
Tied to a flower, a vertical worm,
for fairyfolk to climb –
so, worms, be wary of elf and fairy;
they'll give you a very hard time!

A Wriggly Dip

Dip, dip, earthworm, in the sand,
Who'd like to hold you in their hand?
　Wriggle little earthworm,
　　Wriggle-me-ree,
　　　Will it be the next one?
　　　　No,
　　　　　　not
　　　　　　　　he!

Dip, dip, earthworm, in the sand,
Who'd like to hold you in their hand?
　Wriggle little earthworm,
　　Wriggle-me-ree,
　　　Will it be the next one?
　　　　　　　Yes,
　　　　　　it's
　　　　she!

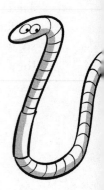

Everyday Worms

rough
worms
tough worms
soft and
sentimental worms
funny
worms
sunny worms
cool, calm and
gentle
worms
worms in the garden
worms in
the park
worms in
the daytime
worms
after
dark
squiggling
wriggling
every
little squirm

just as
individual
as
every
tiny
worm

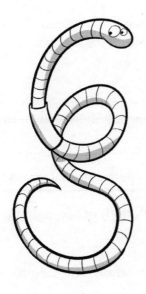

Racing Worms

Humble Worm and Slightly Soiled begin a squirmy race.
They're heading for the compost heap for each to fill their face.

"Last one there's a centipede!" cries Humble, with a grin.
"I'm the fastest worm there is," says Slightly Soiled. "I'll win!"

Humble Worm gets tangled in a labyrinth of roots.
Slightly Soiled surfaces and off the young worm shoots.

Yet wormly pride, the saying goes, comes before a rise:
A blackbird grabs poor Slightly Soiled and lifts him to the skies.

But Slightly Soiled knows stories of what fortune flattery brings;
He keeps his cool and tells the bird how beautifully he sings.

"Of course, I do sing wonderfully!" the foolish blackbird calls:
The plan succeeds – an open beak means Slightly Soiled falls.

This time he wriggles underleaf, quite safe, but not too deep,
And in no time at all he's reached the garden compost heap.

A second later, who arrives, but Humble Worm: "I reckoned
I could beat you, Slightly Soiled, but now I see I'm second."

The worms shake tails and wriggle in the compost for a feed.
"The race was close," says Slightly Soiled, "and I must concede
That you squirmed pretty quickly for – ahem – a centipede!"

A Nonsense Worm

How many worms in a wriggle?
How many wriggles in a squirm?
How many squirms in a flower-bed
if you've only got one worm?

Why Wrinkle Your Nose?

Why wrinkle your nose at poor worms?
They're good creatures, not horrible germs!
They're the gardener's friend,
Turning soil. In the end
Plants grow better because of their squirms.

Charming Worms

I don't mean worms are charming
though, of course, they're rather sweet
and if you're a mole or a hedgehog
then you'll find them good to eat –

no – to 'charm' worms is to tempt them
to come up – let me explain:
you encourage them to surface
when you make them think you're rain.

The poor worms quickly panic
when they feel their ceilings shake,
so they're up and in the sun before
they realise their mistake:

No rain to flood their tunnels!
No worms about to drown!
Just a human with a bucket
who is stamping up and down!

Wiggle, Worm, Wiggle

Worm wiggled under the weeds:
  Wiggle, Worm, wiggle.
Worm wiggled back again.
  Well wiggled, Worm.

Mixed Worms

The garden worm is homely,
he likes bedsock, book and tea.
The field worm is much bolder,
she plays wormball; learns to ski.

The mountain worm's a cool one –
an amazing head for heights!
Woolly sheep and bracken
are among his chief delights.

The seaside worm builds castles
on every sandy shore,
with heaps of curly corridors
but never once a door.

The riverbank worm's bravest,
she's never heard of spud
or carrot, swede or turnip,
all she's ever known is mud.

Worms are all so different
and yet so much the same!
Let's all applaud the gentle worm,
salute its squirmy name.

Cat's Trophy

When cats go out hunting
they'll bring in the house
a frog or a blackbird,
a shrew or a mouse.

When my cat was a kitten
he started out small
and caught a live earthworm
to brighten our hall.

A Close Call

When Hedgehog saw two worms in love
her appetite diminished.
The worms were tangled in a hug
and, when their cuddle finished,

the hedgehog said, "Keep calm, young worms,"
(the worms were looking frantic),
"I cannot eat two worms in love.
I'm just an old romantic."

So if you spot two tangled worms,
locked in a strong embrace,
the chances are you'll also see
a hedgehog's gentle face.

The Worm who was Afraid of the Light

"I don't like it out here on the surface,"
Said a worm to her mother one day.
"It's far too bright. I'm afraid of the light.
Can I please burrow home now and play?"

"Oh, dear! Oh, dear!" said her mother.
"I don't like little worms that wail.
It's a shame that you haven't a house on your back;
You should have been born a snail."

But that gave the worm an idea:
She dressed up in a snail's old shell.
"Look, Mum," called her echoey voice,
"I'm a snail. (But I don't like the smell.)"

Now if you find a shell, listen carefully.
If you hear a small voice saying, "Pooh!"
Then you'll know that there's no snail inside it;
It is occupied by You Know Who!

Squirmy Wormingham

Squirmy Wormingham
Squirmed to Birmingham
   In a shower of rain.
He went for a paddle
Right up to his saddle
   And never went there again.

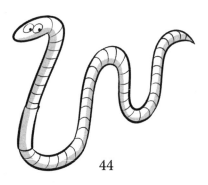

The Wise Old Worm

A wise old worm squirmed under an oak,
The more it saw, the less it spoke.
The less it spoke, the more it learned.
Why aren't we all like that wise old worm?

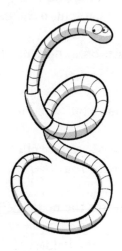

A Prickly Task

Slightly Soiled is slightly scared and here's the reason why:
some ants have seen a dragon in the nettle-bed nearby.

He thinks he might investigate but dares not go alone.
He wriggles off to find his friend but Humble's not at home.

Mrs Worm's a bit concerned, she's heard the rumour, too.
"When you catch up with Humble, please make sure she stays with you."

So off towards the nettle-bed young Slightly starts to squirm,
feeling quite the boldest of the bravest kind of worm.

Soon, as he hides behind a rock, he spots a pair of wings,
big and green and prickly: "The dragon!" Slightly sings.

And though the young worm trembles, it's not quite all he feared:
the dragon isn't scary – it's more a little . . . weird!

Then, when it shakes its spiky wings, its head comes
into view.
Slightly Soiled starts to laugh: "Oh, Humble Worm!
It's you!"

The nettle-bed lies just below a prickly holly tree.
The 'wings' are simply holly leaves on Humble's
back, you see.

She's trying hard to shake them off – they're heavy
and they prick!
But Slightly Soiled soon sets her free with skill (and
one small stick).

"Today I slayed a dragon!" cries Slightly Soiled. He's
proud.
And Humble Worm cries, "So did I!" But, maybe,
not as loud.

Mary Had a Wiggly Worm

Mary had a wiggly worm,
Its face was pink as candy,
And when poor Mary lost her pen
Her worm came in quite handy.

It squirmed with her to school one day
And stayed for half a term,
So Mary dipped it in the ink
And wrote with Wiggly Worm.

More Charming Worms

Though worms enjoy dampness,
life can become too damp,
and that is why they show their heads
should anybody stamp.

Some folk hold competitions
to see who can charm the most:
earthworms, in the country,
or lugworms, at the coast.

And now I see you're thinking:
Why trick the foolish things?
Well, speaking strictly for myself:
to find a worm that sings

And, once they reach the surface,
each worm must take its chance,
but if I find a worm that sings
I'll teach it how to dance.

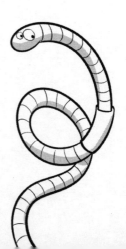

Mr Mole

Mister Mole
He dug a hole
As fast as he could do it.
A worm in the field
Held a stone as a shield
So Moley could not chew it.

Incey Wincey Wormy

Incey Wincey Wormy
Wriggled up a root.
Down came the rain and
On went his boot.

His boot filled with water.
Oh, what a pain!
So Incey Wincey Wormy
Emptied out the rain.

Simple Squirmy

Simple Squirmy met a wormy
  trying to uncoil,
Said Simple Squirmy to the wormy,
  "Let me taste your soil."

Said the wormy to Simple Squirmy,
  "Show me first your leaf."
Said Simply Squirmy to the wormy
  "I lost it to a thief."

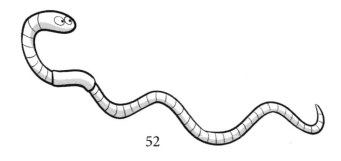

Hickory Dickory Dee

Hickory dickory dee,
A worm squirmed up a tree.
    An apple dropped,
      The poor worm flopped.
Hickory dickory dee.

Hickory dickory doze,
A worm squirmed up a rose.
    It met a spike
      It did not like,
Hickory dickory doze.

Hickory dickory dellie,
A worm squirmed up my wellie.
    I dug up a spud,
      The worm ate the mud,
Hickory dickory dellie.

Wormy Warnings

See a worm, pick it up,
All day long you'll have good luck.
See a worm, let it lie,
You'll eat worms before you die.

More Wormy Warnings

Meet a worm on Monday: have a happy day;
Talk to a worm on Tuesday: trouble on its way;
Wink at a worm on Wednesday: win a lucky bet;
Throw a worm on Thursday: deserve all you get;
Befriend a worm on Friday: look out for a letter;
Stroke a worm on Saturday: something even better;
See a worm on Sunday, and all the week ahead
Worms will be wriggling inside your cosy bed.

Weather Worms

One for sunshine,
Two for showers,
Three for a downpour,
watering the flowers.

Four for a snowflake,
Five for a gale,
Six for a thunderstorm,
lightning and hail.

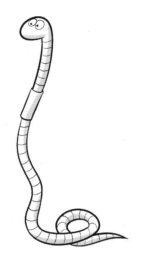

Worms on Ice

It's winter, and the puddles are smooth and hard with ice.
They glisten in the sunshine, so brightly, they entice
Humble Worm and Slightly Soiled to curl up side by side
on one big, shiny laurel leaf: a sledge that lets them slide.

The young worms think it's great to skate
and fail to see it's growing late.
The sun sinks lower in the sky.
The air turns colder – snowflakes fly.

"Oh no! My tail is frozen stiff," cries Slightly Soiled, alarmed.
Humble Worm is freezing, too. Can they survive unharmed?
A sudden shadow overhead makes both worms cry, "What's that?"
A warm and furry feeling helps them realise – it's a cat!

Then, suddenly, a hot, pink sponge gives both the worms a lick.
At once, the worms are warm enough to squirm again – and quick!
They wriggle off their leafy sledge and squiggle off the puddle
to tumble safely down their hole and back home for a cuddle.

Worms in Winter

The north wind doth blow,
And we shall have snow,
And what will the earthworm do then,
              poor thing?

He'll tunnel down deep,
And have a long sleep,
And keep himself warm in his hole,
              poor thing.

Dreams in a Drought

A worm in a drought
digs deep till it rains
while wonderful dreams
fill her tiny brains:

she rides on a rainbow,
  swims seven seas,
gallops on mouseback
  to blackberry trees

she zooms to the moon
  at phenomenal speed
and parachutes home
  on a sycamore seed

And then when the rain comes
she wakes with a smile
drinks deep and will sleep
for another wee while.

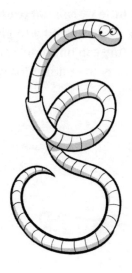

Two Little Worms

Two little worms, all ready for bed:
Giggly Gladys and wriggly Fred.
One tiny cap on each little head,
All ready to cuddle and snuggle in bed.

The Ghost Worm

Sir Wilberforce Worm – a gentleworm, he
lived under the roots of his family tree.

He was born in luxurious lawns facing south,
with a silver-birch leaf, so they say, in his mouth.

On best British oak leaves each night he would dine,
washed down with a goblet of sycamore wine.

Sir Wilberforce Worm was a kind worm and wise,
though now he's long gone to squirm on in the skies

while his wriggly descendants all blissfully boast
that Sir Wilberforce Worm is their ancestral ghost.

And sometimes, at midnight, on dark Halloween
the white misty shape of a worm can be seen:

A shadowy spectre, Sir Wilberforce, he
haunts high leaf and low in his family tree.

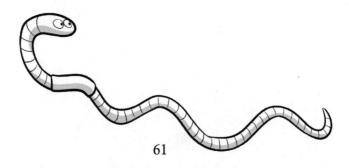

Wee Willie Wormy

Wee Willie Wormy
Squirms round a root,
Upsoil and downsoil,
In his muddy boot,
Squirming to the surface,
Wriggling round a rock,
"Are the worms all underground?
It's past eight o'clock!"

A Worm's Prayer

Before he curls up for the night
an earthworm always prays:
          Keep me safe from hungry mole,
          from rain that floods and drowns.
          May gentle leaves be all that fall
          in reds and golds and browns.
          And whether the soil be sandy,
          or whether the soil be clay,
          may no rough stone confound my hole
          or block my squirmy way.

Rock-a-bye Wormy

Rock-a-bye wormy
safe underground,
When the dog digs
no worm will be found.
When the dog hides
a big, juicy bone,
Wormy keeps sleeping
under a stone.

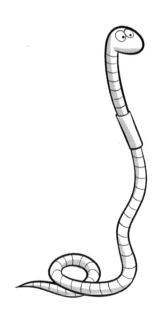